J. I. PACKER ANSWERS QUESTIONS
FOR TODAY

J. I. Packer

J. I. PACKER
ANSWERS QUESTIONS
FOR TODAY

with Wendy Murray Zoba

Tyndale House Publishers, Inc.
Wheaton, Illinois

Visit Tyndale's exciting Web site at www.tyndale.com

Copyright © 2001 by J. I. Packer and Wendy Murray Zoba. All rights reserved.

The authors wish to thank Marshall Shelley and Kevin A. Miller for granting permission to include portions from their interview with J. I. Packer entitled "Children of the Larger God," that appeared in Leadership, Summer 1998.

Material from J. I. Packer, *Growing in Christ*, copyright © 1994 is used by permission of Crossway Books, a division of Good News Publishers, Wheaton, IL 60187.

Material from J. I. Packer, *A Passion for Faithfulness*, copyright © 1995 is used by permission of Crossway Books, a division of Good News Publishers, Wheaton, IL 60187.

Unless otherwise indicated, all Scripture quotations are taken from the *Holy Bible*, New International Version®. NIV®. Copyright © 1973, 1978, 1984 by International Bible Society. Used by permission of Zondervan Publishing House. All rights reserved.

Scripture quotations marked NLT are taken from the *Holy Bible*, New Living Translation, copyright © 1996. Used by permission of Tyndale House Publishers, Inc., Wheaton, Illinois 60189. All rights reserved.

Scripture quotations marked NASB are taken from the *New American Standard Bible*, © 1960, 1962, 1963, 1968, 1971, 1972, 1973, 1975, 1977 by The Lockman Foundation. Used by permission.

Scripture quotations marked RSV are taken from the *Holy Bible*, Revised Standard Version, copyright © 1946, 1952, 1971 by the Division of Christian Education of the National Council of the Churches of Christ in the United States of America, and are used by permission. All rights reserved.

Cover image © Digital Vision, Inc. All rights reserved.

Designed by Julie Chen

Edited by S. A. Harrison and Dan Lins

Library of Congress Cataloging-in-Publication Data

Packer, J. I. (James Innell)
  J. I. Packer answers questions for today / J. I. Packer with Wendy Murray Zoba.
    p.   cm.
  Includes bibliographical references.
  ISBN 0-8423-3615-X (pbk.)
    1. Teenagers—Religious life—Miscellanea. 2. Christian life—Miscellanea. I. Title:
James Innell Packer answers questions for today. II. Zoba, Wendy Murray. III. Title.
BV4531.2.P252000
230—dc21   00-036379

Printed in the United States of America

05 04 03 02 01
6   5   4   3   2   1

CONTENTS

Foreword		vii
Introduction		xi
1	Righting Our Compass	1
2	Getting to Know the Bible	25
3	Drawing Near to God	43
4	Living in Today's World	55
5	Answering Some Hard Questions	73
6	Knowing Packer	87

FOREWORD
By J. I. Packer

Because my wife and I are a one-car couple, I periodically find myself in the bus shelter opposite Regent College waiting for the bus that takes me from work. For some years now the inside back panel of the shelter has carried a two-word message, spray painted in large blue letters: *HELP ME*. I have often wondered who did the painting, and why. The shelter is used by students from the nearby university and from Regent College, and by all sorts of people heading home from the university hospital. Who among them would have gone public with this graffiti item? Was the spray painter on drugs, suffering from alcoholism, depressed, or distressed by a sense of loneliness as one lost in the cosmos? Was that person paralyzed by feelings of inadequacy, fearful of future events, or a victim of some nightmare muddle—perhaps self-created, perhaps not, but certainly destroying life now?

I shall never know, but I can't help wondering and feeling a bit of an ache as I do so. For I am a Christian, and a major part of the Christian's calling is to try to help where help is needed. Beside the message in the shelter, flyers appear from time to time offering academic help and all sorts of social opportunities, but I doubt whether any of that would speak to the spray painter's condition. That message asking for help reminds me that everyone in this world needs the help that only a saving relationship with God can give, which renews my desire to extend that help through sharing the gospel of Jesus Christ every way I can.

This book is a venture in helping, as its title indicates. By trade, Wendy Murray Zoba is a journalist and I am a theologian. But by God-given inclination we both hope to be helpers, and that is what brought us together on this project. It began when Wendy invited me to her home for a rap session with her son Ben and some of his teen peers on questions about Christian living. Wendy taped and transcribed what the questions pulled out of me (it is all in this book, in some form) and suggested publication. The idea grew, and Tyndale House showed interest. It was agreed that more material would make the project helpful to more people, and that it might be helpful, too, to reproduce an article about me that Wendy wrote so that readers might have some idea what sort of a creature it is that mouths these things.

While I hope that people of all ages who seek a fuller knowledge of God will find help here, the target readership is people more than fifty years younger than I am, starting with the upper reaches of Ben Zoba's peer group. Wendy has done the lion's share in midwifing the book into print; readers should therefore join me in thanking her most heartily for her labors.

If I can help somebody
My living will not be in vain.

If this little book helps somebody to gain clarity, grow stronger, and go deeper in his or her Christian faith and life, we, the authors, will feel fully rewarded.

J. I. Packer

INTRODUCTION
by Wendy Murray Zoba

The first time I met J. I. Packer was in December 1994, when my husband and I joined him for breakfast at a local hotel restaurant. He asked, more than once, for hot sauce to put on his eggs. After a second try, when the harried server finally delivered the little red bottle (the eggs by now rubbery), Dr. Packer looked up with that wry British smile and glimmer in his eye and said, "This place has a kind of homespun feel. That's why I like it." I knew, from that moment, that this was a man I needed to learn from.

It is not an exaggeration to say that J. I. Packer rescued my writing career. I had failed at my first attempt to write an essay for CHRISTIANITY TODAY. Then I failed at my *second* attempt to write it. When I went to talk to Jim Packer about it during one of his regular visits to the CT hallway, he said to me, "You got clocked on the head from one side and then you got clocked on the head from the other side" (a Briticism equivalent to, "You got knocked off your horse").

Something more than editorial advice transpired in that meeting. He walked me through the article I was attempting to write, imbuing it with structure, nuance, balance, and devotion—the kind of godly sensibility that enables him to interpret charitably a waitress's rudeness as "homespun" and eat rubbery, though nicely spiced-up, eggs.

It is now standard procedure that before nearly every article I write, I have one such session with J. I. Packer. He helps me see the landscape. He points me in the right direction. He scratches out a road map for getting me where I need to go.

He grounds me. That is his gift. And he brings to bear the same gift in this collaboration. As is evident in the profile I wrote about him (chapter 6, "Knowing Packer," page 87), it is his God-given calling to show people landscapes, to point them in the right direction, and to provide road maps for their journeys. He showed the way when it came to advancing an intellectually cogent evangelicalism in England in the fifties and sixties, when such a thing was hardly heard of. He showed the way again in the seventies and eighties, when American evangelicals struggled to define the "inerrant" nature of the Scriptures. And he is still showing the way.

It is noteworthy that Jim Packer has won the endearing affirmation of my seventeen year-old son, Ben, who sometimes refers to him as "J-I-P-Double-O-C." (Read: J. I. Packer, Out of Control.) Any parent of a teen will tell you that to be referred to as "out of control" is something *good* —not unlike "he's the man"—another of Ben's endearments for him. I bring up my son's fondness for him because it is out of that fondness, and Packer's accessibility, that this book is derived.

Over the years, since that first meeting in 1994, we have enjoyed Jim Packer's company at our dinner table many times. Over chicken tetrazzini one such night, Ben asked him, "Are you a Calvinist?" To which he replied, "Well, Ben, if what you mean by 'Calvinist' is one who believes there is a God who is in control of all that he has made and lovingly attends to his creation, then, yes, I guess you could say that I'm a Calvinist." This was the beginning of an intergenerational bond that highlights, first, how young people long for solid answers about the things of God and, second, how J. I. Packer is able to address this longing with clarity, wit, and spiritual insight.

Ben became a small group leader his junior year in high school. When he learned that Jim Packer would be joining our family for dinner on another occasion, Ben asked, "Do you think he'd come to my small group and talk to the guys?"

"I'll ask him," I said.

Packer said yes, and before that evening was through he had this room full of teenage boys, in equal parts, riveted to his words and howling with laughter.

The idea for this book was spawned as a result of that evening in my living room. But the project expanded and includes Packer's wisdom from a series of other conversations and contexts.

It is our hope and intention that our book will help the searching reader—the reader who has been clocked on the head from one side and then clocked on the head from the other side—who needs to see the landscape of his or her life; who needs to be pointed in the right direction; and who could use a road map for getting where he or she needs to go.

That place, it should be said, is to the center of God's will and plan. And I believe J. I. Packer's wisdom and wit will help you get there.

A WORD FROM BEN ZOBA

When I think of Dr. Packer, I think of 1 Corinthians 11:1, where Paul says, "Follow my example, just as I follow Christ's" (NLT). Dr. Packer has been a great example of a man of God, and I cherish the memories of when he would join our family for dinner, giving me the chance to sit down and talk with him. God's Word says, "Pay attention to my wisdom; listen carefully to my wise counsel" (Prov. 5:1, NLT). That's why, one time when my mom said Dr. Packer was coming to town, I asked her if he would be willing to come and talk to my small group about what it means to be a Christian in this world.

Jesus says, "Whoever wants to be a leader among you must be your servant" (Matt. 20:26, NLT). Dr. Packer obeyed Christ when he took time out of his schedule to sit down with my friends and me and discuss some important questions. Although there was a great age difference between us, we all had a real love for Jesus Christ, which allowed us to be open and understand each other. We guys talked about what was going on in our lives—from dating girls to how to know God's will about which college to attend. He said things like, "Don't marry a goofy girl," and "Don't have any scandalous hobbies." He also told us how we can know God better, and he encouraged us to press on toward the goal and run the race for Christ.

When Dr. Packer was a teen like I am, God showed him that living for Christ was the only thing that would satisfy. Today he is old enough to be my grandpa. It is encouraging to see someone so content in God after a whole lifetime of daily commitment. With his age, God has given Dr. Packer wisdom.

1

RIGHTING OUR
COMPASS

WHY ARE YOU SO DEVOTED TO STUDYING THE BIBLE AND FINDING OUT ABOUT GOD?

When you commit yourself to Christ, you're adopted into the family of Christ's heavenly Father, who now becomes *your* heavenly Father. And when you realize that this means you gain life out of death—and you really do—you feel overwhelmed and find that you very much want to know your heavenly Father as well as you can, and to understand his mind, his will, his plans, and his goals. For that to happen, you have to work with the Bible, which is his Word.

It seems to me that the most natural thing in the world would be that when you are taken into a family, you get interested in the family—particularly in the head of the family. I should be a strange child of God if I wasn't interested in the Bible. I should be showing myself ungrateful for the grace that has brought me into the family and made me a new person and an heir of glory.

When I became a Christian more than half a century ago, I got stuck straight away into soaking up all I could learn about God from the Bible, and that has been a sort of passion with me ever since. Frankly, it still is. Some passions subside as you get older, but not this one.

WHY DO SO MANY PEOPLE FIND THE STUDY OF GOD AND THE BIBLE BURDENSOME AND BORING?

Too often these things have been taught in a rigidly defensive way: "This is the stuff you are to believe and share; these are the errors you are to recognize and reject." Simply projecting orthodoxy that way doesn't give much stimulus to the mind, because the conclusion is determined before you've asked the question. Devotionally it is so barren that even Christians get turned off by it.

Such an approach actually shrinks the soul. Focusing on the greatness of God, though, enlarges the soul. Paradoxically, it makes you a greater person by making you a smaller person. It makes you humble. It lowers you in your own self-estimate. I've always tried to present truth in such a way that it will humble the sinner and exalt the Savior. This produces a Christian who is of larger stature than one who just knows orthodoxy and is prepared to recite it on demand.

**WHAT DOES CHRISTIANITY, WHICH
EXALTS GOD AND DIMINISHES
INDIVIDUAL RIGHTS, OFFER
A CULTURE LIKE OURS THAT AIMS
TO EXALT THE SELF?**

Religion, in many circles, has become the business of trying to make people happy. Anything that enlarges my comfort zone is regarded as good, godly, proper, and to be integrated into my religion.

North American culture, both secular and churchly, zeroes in on the "right to happiness." But a true study of God challenges that notion, for it calls on us to deny claims of self and to exalt God instead. God promises that if we pursue holiness, happiness will come. And it does come, in the form of a joy that the world knows nothing about. Christian self-denial produces more joy and happiness than secular self-indulgence ever does. People who don't know God don't believe that, but it's true.

IS IT LEGITIMATE TO THINK THAT CHRISTIANITY IS A MEANS TO PERSONAL FULFILLMENT?

It is legitimate, once I've guarded myself against the mistake that makes such thinking illegitimate. The mistake is to think of myself as the center of the universe and that God exists for my comfort, convenience, and merely to bless me. That assumption has to be junked. We exist for God. God, in his great mercy, has promised that blessedness will accompany discipleship, but it's got to be God first.

Without that understanding, to say that Christianity is the secret of happiness is dangerous. Often evangelists who preach that way leave the wrong impression and affirm our self-absorption, and then we end up trying Christianity only as a formula for happiness. That kind of teaching is likely to produce substandard saints.

You don't actually help the butterfly emerge from its chrysalis by cutting the chrysalis. If the butterfly doesn't struggle from inside to get out, it comes out as a butterfly that isn't strong enough to fly. People who get into the Christian life without ever being challenged to repent of their self-absorption are, at best, likely to remain stunted as Christians.

DOES THE MATERIALISTIC AND ENTERTAINMENT CULTURE IN NORTH AMERICA IMPEDE OUR ABILITY TO HAVE AN ACTIVE INTEREST IN WHAT IT TRULY MEANS TO BE A CHRISTIAN?

I don't think that this is a North American problem at all. I think it is a human problem and it has been a human problem since the fall. We were all created to be God's image-bearers. That means that we were created to seek and find God through seeking and finding the truth about God. We are made in such a way, I believe, that we are only at peace with ourselves when it's God's truth that our minds are grasping and consciously obeying. Human life is lacking dignity until you get to that point.

IS IT APPROPRIATE TO USE GUILT TO MOTIVATE PEOPLE TO REPENT?

We can't help it. When people wake up to the fact that they've been defying and dishonoring God all these years, they'll feel guilty. The Spirit working in their hearts will see to that! They will know that God is telling them they have lived wrongly, that they must change, and that they need to have the past washed out.

The next question will be, "How can I get straight with God?" This means, "How can I get rid of my guilt?" That's when we can talk about how Christ died for our sins according to the Scriptures; how he redeemed us from the curse of the law by becoming a curse for us.

I hear evangelists say that people today simply don't respond if you teach guilt and then highlight the Cross as God's act of putting away guilt—they don't think of themselves as guilty. Well, if so, that's our fault because we haven't told them of their guilt. We haven't made them recognize how thoroughly they've been dishonoring and defying God. We've left them on the egocentric happiness track. We are wrong to do that.

ISN'T TELLING PEOPLE ABOUT HELLFIRE PASSÉ?

There has been a strong reaction in Christian circles against imaginative presentations of hell, the endless fire and all of that. But people do need to know that lostness is a fact.

My concept of hell owes much to C. S. Lewis, whose key thought is that what you have chosen to be in this world comes back at you as your eternal destiny; if you've chosen to put up the shutters against God's grace rather than receive it, that's how you will spend eternity. Hell is to exist in a state apart from God, where all of the good things in this world no longer remain for you. All that remains is to be shut up in yourself, realizing what you have missed and lost through saying no to God.

In Jean Paul Sartre's play about hell, *No Exit*, four people find themselves in a room they can't leave, and they can't get away from one another. What Sartre presents is the ongoing, endless destruction of each person by the others. Though Sartre was an atheist, his nightmare vision of this process makes substantial sense to me as an image of hell—one aspect of it, anyway. The unending realization of God's displeasure and rejection has to be a reality in hell, too.

HOW DO YOU TALK TO PEOPLE FROM THE BIBLE WHEN THEY MIGHT NOT CARE WHAT THE BIBLE TEACHES?

I haven't got a ready-made formula for doing that. All I know is that when people have a passion to know God and to deepen their relationship with God—just as a chap who's fallen in love has a passion to deepen his relationship with the girl—then everything in Scripture becomes interesting.

I don't know any quick and easy technique for getting people to study the Bible. So I try to preach about the goodness and greatness and glory of God, the Father, the Son, and the Spirit, in a way that I hope will generate the passion. But ultimately, I can't produce that effect. Only the Holy Spirit himself can.

IS IT WRONG TO PRESENT GOD AS THE ANSWER TO ALL OF OUR PROBLEMS? OR, TO PUT IT ANOTHER WAY, IS IT WRONG TO BRING A THERAPEUTIC DIMENSION INTO OUR UNDERSTANDING OF WHO GOD IS?

I don't now believe—indeed I'm not sure I ever believed—that Christians could rely on the Holy Spirit to keep them free from mental and emotional troubles and all need of therapy on that level. The people who convinced me of that were the Puritans. I started reading the Puritans within two years of my conversion. I found that they recognized, straightforwardly, that a lot of people in this world who profess faith will have various kinds of mental and depressive trouble.

As I move around, I do, frankly, find myself shocked and depressed—this is not clinical depression, you understand, merely discouragement—at the amount of feel-good preaching that goes on in Bible-believing churches. I don't believe it can do much good, and I don't believe it can bring much glory to God. It inescapably encourages an ungodly form of the self-centeredness I spoke of earlier: the notion that I and my feelings (which hopefully will be good feelings) are the most important things in the world. It also encourages the idea that God's agenda is to give me good feelings. As a result, if I find that there are no good feelings, it's almost inescapable that I would conclude that God somehow has let me down, has failed, has gone to sleep, or has fallen off his throne. It's a thoroughly unhealthy emphasis.

Again and again God's will for those of us who need healing of body or mind is that, by his strength, we should live with our complaint as long as this life lasts. Remember, the apostle Paul had a "thorn in his flesh," which he asked—three times—to be removed, and it wasn't (2 Cor. 12:7).

WHAT INDICATES THAT A PERSON HAS MOVED FROM SELF-ABSORPTION TOWARD GODLY MATURITY?

Maturity is exemplified by people whom I would characterize as *great souled*. There is a sense of stature, a sense of bigness about them that is directly related to the quality of their discipleship. It gives them dignity, poise, and searching insight. It means that when others abuse them or even martyr them, they generate respect.

Sometimes, though, they generate robust hatred first. Richard Baxter, the seventeenth-century Puritan, is a man I very much admire. He was a man of stature who got under people's skin simply by his poise, passion, and integrity. Just by being a good man and faithfully serving God, he made people feel bad, and they gave him a very hard time as a result.

WHAT PART DOES THE STUDY OF GOD AND THE BIBLE PLAY IN OUR MATURING?

Truth about God and his gracious ways is food for the hungry soul. What we have in the Bible is the raw material, the makings of the meal. We who preach and teach are like the cooks, and it's our business to shape the meal and make it appetizing. Good teaching and preaching will come as a meal for the soul. Thinking over the truth that has been taught or found in our Bible reading—talking to God about it, measuring ourselves by it, and resolving to let it guide our lives—is the process of spiritual digestion. Digesting good meals on a regular basis sets the body on track for growth and maturity, and digesting good spiritual food does the same for the soul. Spiritual anorexia (not taking in the food we need) and spiritual bulimia (not letting ourselves digest it after we have received it, however large the quantities) will keep us from real spiritual health and progress. So it is important not to fall victim to either.

2

GETTING TO KNOW THE BIBLE

SOME PEOPLE SAY THAT THE ACCOUNTS OF THINGS THAT HAPPENED IN THE BIBLE, ESPECIALLY IN CONNECTION WITH JESUS, HAVE LOST ACCURACY THROUGH BEING PASSED FROM MOUTH TO MOUTH— LIKE THE GAME "TELEPHONE," WHERE YOU WHISPER SOMETHING LIKE "BOBBY LIKES SUSIE," AND THE PERSON AT THE END OF THE LINE HEARS IT AS "MY CHEESE IS GREEN." CAN WE TRUST THAT THE BIBLE STORIES ARE ACCURATE?

Well, the first disciples didn't whisper the words and works of Jesus, going over them just once. They preached them to crowds, going over them again and again. And since Jesus' disciples were a close-knit community, all of whom were witnesses to the same events, they could check each others' memories. There's no easy way in which the traditions about Jesus could have gotten twisted out of shape before being written down. Skeptics who are already determined not to believe in Jesus' divinity or miracles say this must have happened, but we don't have to believe them.

The only way that you can respond to these skeptics is to say that all our translations of the Bible have been done by persons of heavyweight academic qualifications—people who know their Hebrew, the language of the Old Testament (with the exception of parts of Daniel which were written in Aramaic), and who know their Greek, the language of the New Testament. And you can add that there is no reason to doubt that biblical books are factually accurate in the history they record, and that the translations are constantly checked by other people who know their Hebrew and Greek and who work from the original languages as they teach these books in colleges and seminaries. How many people have to unite and say that such and such a version is an accurate translation before you'll believe them?

You call the skeptics, in other words, on their attitude—really, on their prejudice. Our generation is blessed more than any generation in any language group anywhere in the world, because we have got something like a dozen *jolly* good English translations of the Bible. No nation or language group has ever had as many trustworthy versions to choose from as we have.

The atmosphere of suspicion that surrounds the questions of skeptics, I think in many cases, is no more than an excuse for them not to take the Bible seriously.

WHICH TRANSLATION IS THE MOST ACCURATE?

Good question. There are about a dozen major English translations, all either good or very good. I find that some people, knowing that there are a lot of translations, get to feeling that this must be because none of them is totally trustworthy. But that's crooked reasoning. In an ice cream parlor you choose the flavor you like best, but all the ice cream, however flavored, is equally good of its kind. The mainstream Bible translations use the English language in different ways, but as translations they can all be trusted, and, overall, are just about as good as each other.

The King James Version was made in 1611. I don't know if you've even tried to read the King James, but if you do, you'll find that it seems to come out of quite a different world from ours, just as Shakespeare does. Majestic and memorable as it is, it uses words in a way that we find old-fashioned and sometimes obscure. All the modern translations are attempts to put the Bible into the sort of English that ordinary folk nowadays speak and understand most clearly.

You ask which are the best ones. Well, it depends who you are. The New International Version (NIV) is, I think, the most widely-used English version at the present time. With it I would bracket the New Living Translation (NLT), a carefully groomed descendant of the Living Bible (TLB). Both the NIV and the NLT are what the grammarians would call a paraphrase. That is to say, neither is a word-for-word translation; both settle constantly for renderings that leave behind the *wording* of the original text in order to express its *force*. But again and again they are really brilliant at getting the substance of the meaning. Both are very easy to read. So is Eugene Peterson's version of the New Testament titled *The Message,* in which paraphrase is pushed to its outer limit with great skill.

There is an older version which is, on the whole, very accurate and clear, though sometimes rather low-key. It follows closely the wording of the Hebrew and Greek and expresses this in very straightforward English. That is the Revised Standard Version (RSV), which also appears in a slightly revised form as the English Standard Version (ESV). The New King James Version (NKJV) and the New American Standard Bible (NASB) are also impressive as literal, word-for-word renderings. Ideally, I think we all should have (and use) two English Bibles, one of each type.

I could go on rating them all, but these are the main ones.

YOU SAID THAT JESUS' FOLLOWERS "PREACHED" THE WORDS AND DEEDS OF JESUS. WHEN DID THEY DECIDE IT SHOULD ALL BE WRITTEN DOWN?

We have four Gospels containing stories and words of Jesus. The great majority of the people who study these things will assure you that those Gospels were written between about A.D. 50 and A.D. 90. They differ among themselves as to precisely when within that forty-year period Matthew, Mark, Luke, and John wrote their books, and certainty on that seems unattainable. But we should not therefore doubt the records themselves. The point I'm making is that the four Gospels were written in the generation following the time when Jesus was alive. Written, that is, in the lifetime of many of the men and women who had been his followers before his crucifixion, and who therefore could check the accuracy of the accounts.

It was a culture in which memory was regularly relied upon and the people were taught to memorize. They didn't write down notes very much. But they did memorize like crazy. With that, however, like us, they also wrote letters, agreements, and whole books, so that important information would be permanently available in an accurate form. The church's mission of worldwide evangelism, as well as its own worship, required that the facts about Jesus be made available this way. Before our four Gospels were composed, there's reason to believe that many people were already writing down the words and works of Jesus (see Luke 1:1-4) and, as I said, the people who had been his disciples—especially the faithful eleven, all of whom were probably young men in, or hardly beyond, their twenties—memorized his sayings and had been unable to forget his doings. So we can be confident that what we have in the Gospels is a trustworthy tradition.

If I, a man now in my seventies, can still vividly recall my university days and the second World War—and I can—I refuse to believe that the true facts about Jesus could have been totally lost or hopelessly mangled before the Gospels were put together. The idea is nonsense.

In the worlds of scholarship and academic teaching, there are always one or two freaks who will take way-out positions. At the present time, there are some scholarly oddities who are skeptical about most of what's in the Gospels. You might have heard of the Jesus Seminar, which is a sort of rallying point for a number of them. But they are only a small group. As one who moves around in the world of professional biblical study, I can tell you that the majority of established scholars have no doubt that the substance of the four Gospels can be trusted. Every rational consideration points that way.

THE OLD TESTAMENT IS MORE COMPLICATED. HOW CAN WE KNOW THAT IT IS TRUSTWORTHY?

Here, too, there are always the people who are resolved to be skeptical. But the fact is that the Old Testament history books hang together. They tell a single story. They add up. From the details they contain, they show every sign of being authentic representations of the way things were and of what went on in the time they are written about. This is as true of the records of the patriarchs and Moses as it is of the time of the kings, the period when the Jews were exiled, and the time of their return. In other words, there's no objective reason for doubting the historical truth of the Old Testament and every reason for assuming it.

It ought to be said, before we move on, that while history is the backbone of the Bible, telling as it does how our Creator became our Redeemer, both Testaments are more than simply records of things that happened. Both contain revelations from God—messages to prophets and others, plus the teaching of God-made-flesh in the person of Jesus. They both are full of *theology*, that is, God-given truth about God's will, work, and ways, and about the practice and problems of godliness. This is taught by the way facts, events, and characters are presented in narrative passages; by interpretive comments sprinkled through the stories; by the sermons in letter form that came from the apostles; and by the prosaic and poetical perspectives on life offered by the Old Testament wisdom writing. (It has been well said of these writings that the Psalms teach how to praise and pray, Proverbs teaches how to live, the Song of Solomon teaches how to love, Job teaches how to suffer, and Ecclesiastes teaches how to enjoy.) If you want your knowledge of the Bible to lead you to personal knowledge of God, you must explore, not just the history, but the theology, too.

HOW SHOULD A BEGINNING BIBLE READER APPROACH READING IT?

I would say start with the Gospels—Matthew, Mark, Luke, John. They tell about Jesus. Reading them, you watch and hear Jesus in action. The reason they are called Gospels is that the *gospel*—the saving truth about Jesus as Savior and Lord—is carefully set forth in each of them, by their selection and arrangement of material. So they really are the most precious books in the Bible, indeed in the world. Read them often! Then go to the Acts of the Apostles, which comes right after the Gospels, in which you watch the first followers of Jesus spreading the Word. Go on from there to the shorter of the letters, or epistles, as they're called. In the letters you've got people like the apostles Paul and John and Peter writing as pastors to churches and groups of people who are disciples like us. They are telling them in broad terms how to live as faithful followers of Christ and children of the heavenly Father. The longer letters, though powerful and profound, are more demanding and easier to get lost in, so save them till later. Read the Old Testament by the light of the New, which presents new life in Jesus as what the Old Testament was leading up to. The key books here are Genesis, Exodus, Isaiah, and the Psalms.

But while you're getting all that stuff under your belt, you need to take full advantage of the preaching and teaching that your church offers, plus the wisdom of friends who can help you understand what's in the Bible. At the beginning of your Christian life, it's rather important that you take full advantage of what you can learn in fellowship with other Christians, because the Bible comprises fourteen-hundred pages of very small print. It takes time to get abreast of all that.

HOW CAN A PERSON DEVELOP A PATTERN FOR BIBLE READING THAT WILL HELP HIM OR HER KNOW GOD BETTER?

I don't claim to be an expert in this field, but I've been teaching for many years, and I try to practice for myself, a procedure that goes like this:

One: Before you open your Bible, remember you are in the presence of God. Remind yourself that God is the primary author of Scripture and that what you are seeking is the personal togetherness that you would hope for if you were opening a letter from someone you knew cared for you. Remember that and think of it consciously before you do anything else. Then ask God to speak to you, and make you listen, as you read.

Two: You begin to read. I urge that *all* the Bible should be read, and read regularly. You and I should acquaint ourselves with the full landscape of Scripture and keep covering it backwards and forwards. Something like four chapters a day, I find, is a very good plan. It gets you through the whole Bible in approximately a year.

Three: Focus particularly on the richer books. This is quite distinct from point two. There are some books in Scripture which, as words from God to his people, have a richer vitamin content than others.

The four Gospels in which you see your Lord in action, as we saw a moment ago, are the most precious books in the world. They are the Bible books that ought to be read oftener than any others. I also think the Psalter ought to be read regularly, one or two psalms every day as a minimum. (Treat Psalm 119 as a cluster of twenty-two 8-verse psalms for this purpose.) There are different sorts of psalms: some are praises, some are petitions, some are songs of complaint; others are a mixture of celebration and intercession with the psalmist looking back on the great things God has done for him and for others, and drawing encouragement from that. You should try to find the condition of heart in the Psalter that matches your own inner experience and make it your own day by day. If your heart is full of praise, well, that shouldn't be too difficult, because many psalms are written that way. If your heart is full of distress, sanctify your complaints by laying them before God as you pray through the complaint psalms. Intercession in some psalms draws its boldness from the memory of how God has blessed in the past, so at that point review your own past experience of God's goodness. If you find the psalmists' exuberance, intensity, sudden shifts of theme, and utter lack of inhibitions too much for you at first, don't be discouraged. These men were more alive in themselves and in God than most of us are, and it takes time to catch up with them. (It took me about twenty years from my conversion before I could feel I was on their wavelength; I hope you will get on faster than I did.)

Four: Linger in those books that have a special resonance with you individually. One book which I have found wonderfully enriching to read over and over is Paul's letter to the Romans.

The way Paul strings things together is the model of what a systematic study of God's saving activity ought to be. It's all there. The fifth century Bishop of Antioch, John Chrysostom, had somebody read the letter to the Romans aloud to him once every week. I can understand that.

So, to reiterate. Point one: come humbly into the presence of God. Point two: read all of Scripture generally. Point three: focus on the richer books—among which, it seems to me, the Gospels and the Psalms are especially significant. Point four: linger in those books that have a special resonance with you individually.

WHAT IS YOUR FAVORITE BOOK OF THE BIBLE?

Most often, I go back to the ten-page wisdom tract called Ecclesiastes, which is the Greek word for "preacher," but can also mean teacher, spokesman, philosopher, or pundit. Sheer bracing delight is the reason: Ecclesiastes does me good. What he says, sadly and beautifully, about the pain of brainwork (the more you know, the more it hurts), about the boredom of the supposedly interesting and the hollowness of acclaimed achievement (all pointless! like trying to grasp the wind!), about the crazy-quilt character of life, about our ignorance of what God is up to, and about death as life's solitary certainty, grabs me deep down. I felt all this as an adolescent, and I still do.

What he says about life's best being an enjoyment of the basics—one's work, meals, marriage—makes me want to laugh and cheer, for this, too, is what I have felt all my adult life. My built-in makeup as an anti-Pollyanna, reality man anchors me in Ecclesiastes' corner, where realism is the name of the game. I know, of course, that feelings, in the sense of emotionally charged intuitions—especially gloomy ones—can be quite unrealistic. So it gives me a large charge to find that some of my own deepest reactions belong to biblical wisdom.

The text that runs most constantly around my heart is Ecclesiastes' exit line: "Here is the conclusion of the matter: Fear God and keep his commandments, for this is the whole duty of man," meaning everybody. "For God will bring every deed into judgment, including every hidden thing, whether it is good or evil" (Eccles. 12:13-14). In the face of life's randomness and bitterness, says the writer, I must keep worshiping God and doing what I have been told to do—then I can't go wrong. God is very concerned that I would keep on keeping on in the godly life, no matter what.

The statement is really a bassoon version in Old Testament terms of Paul's trumpets-and-drums declaration in 1 Corinthians 15:58: "Be steadfast, immovable, always abounding in the work of the Lord, knowing that your toil is not *in* vain in the Lord" (NASB). So, Ecclesiastes helps me hear Paul, and Paul helps me understand Ecclesiastes. With these twin texts echoing in my ears, I go on my way rejoicing.

3

DRAWING NEAR TO GOD

WHAT DOES IT MEAN TO "CHOOSE JESUS"?

The phrase might suggest it is like choosing the preferred dish from a menu—a choice where you opt for what strikes you as the best of the bunch, knowing that if your first choice is not available, a second is always possible. But coming savingly to Christ is not like that. When it occurs, there is a sense of inevitability about it, springing from three sources. First, there is the pressure of the gospel truth that feels too certain to be denied; second, there is the sense of God's presence forcing one to face the reality of Jesus Christ; and third, there is the realization that without him, one is lost. This sense is generated by God's action of making the first move, what we call *prevenient grace* (meaning the prompting of the Holy Spirit). There is no commitment to Christ—no "choice for Jesus," if one prefers to say it that way—apart from this convicting divine action.

The act of the heart in choosing Jesus Christ is not always performed in a single moment, nor is it always performed calmly and clearheadedly. At the surface level there are often crosscurrents of reluctance. C. S. Lewis, dissecting his own conversion story, wrote of "the steady, unrelenting approach of him whom I so earnestly desired not to meet." He scoffed at the idea that anyone who is not a believer, no matter how religiously inclined, really seeks the real God and the real, living Christ, with their dominating, dictatorial demands for discipleship. ("You might as well speak of the mouse's search for the cat.") But in every real conversion, prevenient grace ensures a real change of heart through the irresistible Calvary love of Christ. Then you not only acknowledge the Savior's reality, but you speak to him and embrace him and hand yourself over to him, not just because you know you should, but because you want to. Isaac Watts put it into verse this way:

> *My dear almighty Lord,*
> *My Conqueror and my King,*
> *Thy scepter and Thy sword,*
> *Thy reigning grace I sing:*
> *Thine is the power; behold, I sit*
> *In willing bonds before Thy feet.*

CAN GOD LOVE ME EVEN WHEN I HAVE DONE SO MANY BAD THINGS?

Sin is everybody's problem in the sight of God. He is "of purer eyes than to behold evil," and cannot "look on wrong" (Hab. 1:13, RSV). Sin is a perversity touching each one of us at every point in our lives. Except for Jesus Christ, no human being has ever been free of its infection. The Anglican Prayer Book rightly teaches: "We have followed too much the devices and desires of our own hearts.... We have left undone those things which we ought to have done, and we have done those things which we ought not to have done, and (spiritually) there is no health in us."

The good news, however, is this: sins can be forgiven. Central to the gospel is the glorious "but" of Psalm 130:3-4, "If you, O LORD, kept a record of sins, O Lord, who could stand? *But* with you there is forgiveness; therefore you are feared" (emphasis mine). If our sins were unforgivable, where would we be? A bad conscience delivering at full strength, tearing you to pieces in the name of God, is hell indeed.

Martin Luther, the Reformer, writing to a friend who was distressed about his sin, said, "Learn to know Christ and him crucified. Learn to sing to him and say, 'Lord, you are my righteousness, I am your sin. You took on you what is mine; you set on me what is yours.'"

Link up with Jesus, the living Lord, by faith, and this great exchange is fulfilled. Through Jesus' atoning death, God accepts you as righteous and cancels your sins.

IS IT A REQUIREMENT THAT CHRISTIANS GO TO CHURCH?

As proverbially as we say to each other, "Love me, love my dog," so our Lord says to us all, "Love me, love my church." Something is wrong with professed Christians who do not identify with the church, love it, invest themselves in it, and carry its needs on their hearts. Listen to Paul instructing the Ephesian believers: "Christ loved the church and gave himself up for her to make her holy, cleansing her by the washing with water through the word, and to present her to himself as a radiant church" (Eph. 5:25-27).

But how should our love for the church be focused and expressed? The New Testament sees the church as the Lord's people getting together on a regular basis to praise and pray, with preaching and teaching; to practice fellowship and pastoral care, with mutual encouragement and accountability; to exalt and honor Jesus Christ, specifically by word (preaching), song, and the rituals of communion and baptism; and to reach out, locally and cross-culturally, in order to share Christ with people who need him. Here, love for the church finds expression in a constant quest for faithfulness, holiness, and vitality—ardor animating order—in the corporate life of fellowshiping with the Father and the Son through the Spirit. Yes, all we who believe are meant to be part of this.

WHY ARE THERE DIFFERENT DENOMINATIONS?

When today we in the West speak of "our church," we are normally referring either to the building, a roofed meeting hall, auditorium, or worship space, sometimes towered or steepled; or to the denomination, a federation of like-minded or at least like-mannered congregations. The New Testament, however, knows nothing of church buildings, nor of denominations (understanding these as congregations maintaining, alongside the universal Christian basics, some distinctives of secondary importance—doctrinal, ethical, disciplinary, ethnic, or whatever—and treating themselves as a family unit within the larger family of God). Denominations are an inescapable fact of today's Christianity and have, on occasion, proved their value by standing for truths others were forgetting. But when Jesus spoke of "my church," what he had in view was a worldwide community unified and identified by a shared allegiance to himself; a common acknowledgment of his claim upon them and his lordship over them; and a common bond of love, loyalty, and devotion to him. Local congregations fit into this concept as small-scale expressions of the one church's ongoing life. Denominations are not part of the idea at all.

COULD GOD BRING SOMEONE TO THE POINT OF SAVING FAITH WITHOUT THEM EVER HEARING THE GOSPEL?

The question is prompted by the apostle Peter's statement: "God does not show favoritism but accepts men from every nation who fear him and do what is right" (Acts 10:34-35). It is supported by Paul's assertion that God "has not left himself without testimony" (Acts 14:17). Add to that his strong declaration of God revealing himself generally to all humanity in Romans 1:18-2:16. As it says in Romans 1:20, "Since the creation of the world God's invisible qualities—his eternal power and divine nature—have been clearly seen, being understood from what has been made, so that men are without excuse." The idea that God will judge us all according to what we have done with the light we were given (and that that is supremely just on his part), I take for granted.

In *Christianity and World Religions*, the late Sir Norman Anderson states the question as it relates to non-Christian worshipers: "Might it not be true of the follower of some other religion that the God of all mercy had worked in his heart by his Spirit, bringing him in some measure to realize his sin and need for forgiveness, and enabling him, in his twilight as it were, to throw himself on God's mercy?"

The answer seems to be yes, it might be true. Who are we to deny it? If ever it is true, such worshipers will learn in heaven that they were saved by Christ's death and that their hearts were renewed by the Holy Spirit. They will join the glorified church in endless praise of the sovereign grace of God. Christians since the second century have hoped so, and perhaps Socrates and Plato are in this happy state even now—who knows?

But we have no warrant to affirm categorically that this is true in the sense of having actually happened to people to whom God's promises never came; nor are we entitled to expect that God will act thus in any single case where the gospel is not known or understood. Therefore our missionary obligation is not one whit diminished by our entertaining this possibility.

If we are wise, we shall not spend much time mulling over Sir Norman's notion. Our job, after all, is to spread the gospel, not to guess what might happen to those whom it never reaches. Dealing with them is God's business. He is just and also merciful, and when we learn, as one day we shall, how he has treated them, we shall have no cause to complain. In the meantime, let us keep before our minds humanity's universal need of forgiveness and new birth, and the graciousness of the "whosoever will" invitations of the gospel. And let us redouble our efforts to make known the Christ who saves all who come to God by him.

4

LIVING IN
TODAY'S WORLD

HOW CAN I KNOW THE WILL OF GOD FOR MY LIFE?

First, be sure that you have the basic relationship with God—that is, that you are converted, that you are committed to Jesus, that you are in the family of God, and that God is your Father. It would be pointless to worry about knowing the will of God if you're not related to him.

Then, go to the Bible. If you don't know your Bible very well, get to know somebody who does and ask for help. God never intended that we should all go into our separate corners and invent Christianity for ourselves just by reading the Bible on our own.

To answer the question more specifically, I come back and ask, "What particularly do you want to know?" God in Scripture gives particular teaching about the particularities of every Christian's life. If the question means, "How can I get foolproof inner signals from God to control every decision I ever make" or, "How can I get a preview of what is in store for me over the next fifty or seventy years" then it is a wrong question, asking for something God nowhere promises to give. I hope that it really means, "How am I to organize my days and plan my career and so on, so as to please God by the way I square up to life's challenges?"

Well, Scripture lays down a primary requirement: that we worship with God's people, which means his church on Sunday. And then, when we're thinking about the things we do, that we stay within the limits of biblical propriety. Keep clear of impurity and other things that transgress the basic moral law. You can't go to church very long, nor seriously read your Bible, without learning what these things are.

And then, do everything that you take in hand as well as you can, because that is the way God wants us to live. Never let the good be the enemy of the best. Never settle for being half-hearted where you might be wholehearted. Christian living is meant to be wholehearted living. To put it in words from Ecclesiastes: "Whatever your hand finds to do, do it with all your might" (Eccles. 9:10).

What more can I say? Keep asking your Christian friends, peers, and seniors, "What's your take on this question?" when you're not certain what is the best and most biblical thing to do in relation to something that demands decision. And regularly ask God to block and thwart any mistaken decisions or commitments that he sees you have made.

CAN THE BIBLE TELL ME WHICH COLLEGE TO GO TO?

All through the Bible we are told to seek wisdom. Wisdom means that you aim at the best goal, and follow the best way to get to your goal. As I said, never let the good be the enemy of the best. Look then for the college that will give you the best all-round education, the best start. If you're particularly good at a sport, look for a college where you will get the best coaching. Common sense? Yes, exactly! The Bible makes it a rule for the Christian life to seek wisdom all the time and try always to make wise decisions. Common sense is a regular element in those decisions. Where you should aim to go to college is one example of where a wise decision is called for, but there are others. The time will come (and I'm talking to the young men here) when you will date and wonder, *Is this the girl that I want to marry?* Well, when that happens, just check that she'd be a good partner, because some girls who are nice to look at would never make a good partner. They're wild, or at least not sensible. Don't marry a goofy girl, because there's no future in it. Ask someone who knows you both whether you would be good for each other and think seriously about the reply you get. That's wisdom! I kid you not.

And let me add, loud and clear, that this wisdom should guide young women, as well. Don't marry a young man who is childish, silly, irresponsible, macho, or crazy about material things; he won't be good for you, and though you may dream of changing and improving him (women do so dream), you are not likely to be able to. Don't take risks with men you can't respect.

Getting back now to the point: We're talking in general terms about doing the will of God. If you make the most sensible decision—the wisest decision in any situation—you'll be on track. And you should take your decisions back to God and say, "Lord, I've worked it out as best I can and have tried to make the best decision. If what I've decided is right, please confirm it with peace in my heart. If, for any reason I haven't decided right, please disturb me and prevent me from going ahead where I'm wrong."

I have been a Christian over fifty years and have been working with the Bible as best I can all that time. I have come to believe that there just isn't a problem about how to serve and please God which isn't dealt with in the Bible somewhere, at a wisdom level.

HOW SHOULD WE VIEW SECULAR ENTERTAINMENT SUCH AS MUSIC, MOVIES, AND TELEVISION?

All work and no play makes Jack a dull boy. That's an old British proverb, and it's true. If there's no place in your life for fun, people will find you wearisome company. I don't want to recommend that you travel that road at all. God isn't against entertainment. But it had better be decent stuff that entertains you. What I mean is, it should be of the sort for which you can honestly thank God because you know that it's OK by him. We have to understand that the purpose of fun and games and entertainment is to achieve the goal of rest and refreshment: in other words, to psych you up for the next bit of serious work. Recreation is to become re-creation, a means of renewing energy for life's main tasks. Don't let entertainment become the biggest thing in your life. There are more important things than entertainment.

There's lots of entertainment that's genuine fun, genuine delight. Music can be very invigorating. Martin Luther, the Reformer, said that next to Christ, music is God's best gift to man. In his moments of rest he would play the flute and sing. Well, if you've got music running in your bones like Martin Luther had, you will play and sing too. That's good. But don't let it get out of proportion. You can let music get on top of you, even becoming a slave to music. Actually, if you become a slave to anything, that's a sign that you ought to pull back from it. We're supposed to be slaves—that is, totally committed servants—only to the Lord Jesus and to our heavenly Father.

HOW CAN I TELL IF I'M SPENDING TOO MUCH TIME ON ENTERTAINMENT?

The principle that applies here is the Sabbath principle of six days' work followed by one day's rest. That gives a proportion of one to six, which means that recreational entertainment may properly take up something like fifteen percent of your time.

Think it through in terms of an ordinary day. You're going to do an ordinary day's work. There's nothing inappropriate about one to two hours of entertainment. One, probably, most days, rather than two, and a bit more on weekends.

Don't become a couch potato and sit watching the television for six or eight hours at once. That's letting entertainment get out of hand, and it takes the bloom off all your life. You miss the pleasure of doing things for yourself—hard work, creative hobbies, good sport. It would be very unwise if you let that happen to you.

Other things being equal, the creative hobbies are the most fulfilling ones. So if you're a performer on a musical instrument, you'll get a lot more fun out of that than from watching television. And actually playing a sport is likely to give you more joy than spectating. Though, I grant you, spectating can be fun—especially when your team is winning.

IS IT ALL RIGHT FOR CHRISTIANS TO WATCH R-RATED MOVIES IF THEY ARE NOT "R" FOR NUDITY AND VIOLENCE, BUT FOR CONTENT?

The first thing to ask there is whether I really need to see the movie in order to appreciate the point that it's making. If you think that you do, ask the Lord that you'll get good from the film and that the messy stuff won't mess you up. Ask him for that in prayer before you go, and in prayer tell him what you thought of it when you come out.

This actually illustrates a practical principle which is very important for a Christian: You share everything with the Lord. You seek his blessing in everything that you do. You try to keep out of your life things that you can't offer to him and thank him for. And you discuss with him the life experiences that he's given you and ask him regularly, "Lord, what should I learn from this?" That's down-to-earth, nitty-gritty Christianity.

HOW DO WE STRIKE THE RIGHT BALANCE BETWEEN HONORING GOD IN OUR ACTIVITIES AND STILL REACHING OUT TO NON-CHRISTIANS?

We are in the world in order to love and help people and try to lead them to share our faith. That means making friends with people who aren't Christians—a good thing to do. All of us ought to seek from God a gift of friendship with fellow human beings who are not yet Christians. Being able to build quick relationships with other people so that they'll open their hearts to you and you can open your heart to them, it seems to me, is a spiritual gift which makes it natural and easy to share with them the things that are most precious to you as a believer. In that activity we can certainly honor God. Honest friendship, as I said, is a lovely Christian thing.

The problem behind this question might be, how do we proportion our time so that other God-honoring activities to which we are already committed do not get neglected while we reach out to non-Christians? The guiding principle here is to be realistic, and do not bite off more than you can chew. Make sure you meet existing obligations (schoolwork, part-time and full-time jobs, tasks at home, family responsibilities, or whatever) before you take on new ones, even in evangelism. Day by day and week by week, plan how you will spend your time.

HOW INVOLVED SHOULD WE BE IN THE ACTIVITIES OF NON-CHRISTIANS AS WE TRY TO BUILD FRIENDSHIPS?

It's difficult to answer the question as you put it, because it's so broad. Paul, on one occasion (1 Cor. 5:9-10), said to the people to whom he was writing (to paraphrase), "I'm not telling you to have nothing to do with people who aren't Christians and who live immorally, because that would mean you'd have to go out of the world." Which, of course, you can't do.

But the general idea which that word *world* expresses relates to people in the community organized apart from God and often against God. And the question, as I take it, really means, how deeply do you get involved in activities that are godless and sometimes anti-god in character?

The answer has to be that we don't get committed to such activities, not ever. That means sometimes you must stand apart from a gang of people who are going off together to do something that is dubious. Groups of chaps will go off on Saturday night with the sole purpose of getting drunk or getting stoned or getting laid. The Christian simply doesn't join in parties like that. And if asked why not, the answer is, "This isn't the way that my Lord wants me to live. So if you don't mind, I'm not coming."

Sometimes they do mind, of course, and you make yourself

unpopular because you won't join in. There are places in Scripture that describe how people get surprised and upset when you won't do the things that they're going to do, which they know are wrong (see, for instance, 1 Pet. 4:1-4). Some people feel that if they do something in a group that would be wrong for them as individuals, it somehow becomes all right. It's the gang mentality. It happens with people of all ages, all over the world.

What we all have to do is to try and ensure that everything that we take part in is honorable and will please the Lord, so that we can offer it to him and ask him to bless us in it.

WHAT WOULD BE YOUR "ADVICE FOR LIFE" THAT YOU WISH YOU HAD HEARD AS A YOUNG PERSON?

Just this, the only thing that will make sense out of your lives is to faithfully follow the Lord Jesus. For time and eternity, he's the one to hang onto. So whatever else you do, make sure that you know and love and trust and obey him.

It's very elementary to say that, but the rule of wisdom is always to begin at the beginning. That's the beginning. All through life, walking with Jesus and pleasing Jesus will be linked up with what we spoke of earlier—trying in everything to honor your heavenly Father. You honor the Father by honoring the Son. That's the lodestar for guiding your life, the magnetic north for your compass, if you like to put it that way. I was eighteen before anyone said that to me. I wish I had been told it long before.

5

ANSWERING SOME
HARD QUESTIONS

WILL A LOVING GOD REALLY CONDEMN PEOPLE TO HELL?

The problem of individual human destiny has always pressed hard upon thoughtful Christians who take the Bible seriously, for Scripture affirms these three things: (1) The *reality* of hell as a state of eternal, destructive punishment, in which God's judgment for sin is directly experienced; (2) the *certainty* of hell for all who choose it by rejecting Jesus Christ and his offer of eternal life; and (3) the *justice* of hell as an appropriate divine judgment upon humanity for our lawless and cruel deeds.

It was, to be sure, hell-deserving sinners whom Jesus came to save. All who put their trust in him may know themselves forgiven, justified, and accepted forever—and thus delivered from the wrath to come. But what of those who lack this living faith—those who are hypocrites in the church; or "good pagans" who lived before Christ's birth; or those who, through no fault of their own, never heard the Christian message, or who met it only in an incomplete and distorted form? Or what of those who lived in places where Christianity was a capital offense, or who suffered from ethno-nationalistic or sociocultural conditioning against the faith, or who were so resentful of Christians for hurting them in some way that they were never emotionally free for serious thought about Christian truth? Are they all necessarily lost?

The universalist idea that all people will eventually be saved by grace is a comforting belief. It relieves anxiety about the destiny of pagans, atheists, devotees of non-Christian religions, victims of post-Christian secularity—the millions of adults who never hear the gospel and the millions of children who die before they can understand it. All sensitive Christians would like to embrace universalism. It would get us off a very painful hook.

However, no biblical passage unambiguously asserts universal final salvation, and some speak very explicitly about the lostness of the lost. Universalism is a theological speculation that discounts the meaning of these New Testament passages in favor of what Universalists claim to be the thrust of New Testament thinking: that is, that God's retributive justice toward humanity is always a disciplinary expression of love that ultimately wins them salvation.

It would be nice to believe that, but Scripture nowhere suggests it when speaking of judgment, and the counterarguments seem overwhelmingly cogent. Universalism ignores the constant biblical stress on the *decisiveness* and *finality* of this life's decisions for determining eternal destiny. "God 'will give to each person according to what he has done.' To those who by persistence in doing good seek glory, honor and immortality, he will give eternal life. But for those who are self-seeking and who reject the truth and follow evil, there will be wrath and anger. There will be trouble and distress for every human being who does evil.... but glory, honor, and peace for everyone who does good.... For God does not show favoritism" (Rom. 2:6-11). This is Paul affirming God's justice according to the classic definition of justice, as giving everyone his or her due. All Scripture speaks this way.

Universalism condemns Christ himself, who warned people to flee hell at all costs. If it were true that all humanity will ultimately be saved from hell, he would have to have been either *incompetent* (ignorant that all were going to be saved) or *immoral* (knowing, but concealing it, so as to bluff people into the kingdom through fear).

The Universalist idea of sovereign grace saving all nonbelievers after death raises new problems. If God has the ability to bring all to faith eventually, why would he not do it in this life in every case where the gospel is known? If it is beyond God's power to convert all who know the gospel here, on what grounds can we be sure that he will be able to do it hereafter? The Universalist's doctrine of God cannot be made fully coherent.

Universalism, therefore, as a theory about destiny, will not work. This life's decisions must be deemed to be decisive. And thus, proclaiming the gospel to our fallen, guilty, and hell-bent fellows must be the first service we owe them in light of their first and basic need. "I am obligated both to Greeks and non-Greeks. . . . to preach the gospel," wrote Paul. "For 'every one who calls on the name of the Lord will be saved.' How, then, can they call on the one . . . of whom they have not heard? . . . Faith comes from hearing the message, and the message is heard through the word of Christ" (Rom. 1:14-15; 10:13-14, 17; see Joel 2:32).

HEBREWS 9:27 SAYS, "MAN IS DESTINED TO DIE ONCE, AND AFTER THAT TO FACE JUDGMENT." CAN SOMEONE WHO HAS DIED BE CONVERTED AFTER PHYSICAL DEATH?

When the writer of Hebrews speaks of dying "once," he uses a word that means "once and for all"; not once as distinct from two or more times. By happening once, the event changes things permanently so that the possibility of it happening again is removed. That is what the word means when it is applied in verses 26 and 28 to Jesus' atoning sacrifice on the Cross.

The unrepeatable reality of physical death leads directly to reaping what we sowed in this world. This is what Jesus taught in his tale of the callous rich man and Lazarus the beggar (Luke 16:19-31), and when he spoke of dying in one's sin as something supremely dreadful (John 8:21-23). And this is what Paul taught when he affirmed that, on judgment day, all will receive a destiny corresponding to their works. The New Testament is solid in viewing death and judgment this way.

Modern theologians are not all solid here. Some of them expect that some who did not embrace Christ in this life may yet do so savingly in the life to come. Some link with this the idea that the God of grace owes everyone a clear presentation of the gospel in terms they understand, which is certainly more than many receive in this life. Others, like the Universalists mentioned earlier, presume all humans will finally enjoy God in heaven, and therefore that God must and will continue to exert loving pressure, one way or another, till all have been drawn to Christ. The late Nels Ferre described hell as having "a school and a door" in it—when those in hell come to their senses about Christ, they may leave, so that place ends up empty. But this is non-scriptural speculation and reflects an inadequate grasp of what turning to Christ involves.

How a newly-dead person's perceptions differ from what they were before death is more than we have been told. But Scripture says nothing of prevenient grace triggering postmortem conversions. That being so, we should conclude that the unbeliever's lack of desire for Christ and the Father and heaven before death remains unchanged after death. For God to extend the offer of salvation beyond the moment of death, even for thirty seconds, would be pointless. Nothing would come of it.

IF JESUS WAS GOD IN THE FLESH, HOW DO WE EXPLAIN HIS DEATH? CAN THE ETERNAL GOD DIE?

The background to this question is today's post-Christian perplexity as to whether physical death is the end of the person who lived in (or, more accurately, through) the now-defunct body.

All brands of materialists—scientific, philosophical, theoretical Marxist, secular irreligious, and antireligious European and American—say physical death is the end. Everyone else, from ancient Egyptians, Greeks, and Norsemen to every form of religion and tribal culture the world has ever seen, has been sure it isn't. Historic, Bible-based Christianity is part of this latter consensus. On the nature of postmortem life there are great differences of opinion, but on its reality, agreement has been so widespread that current Western skepticism about survival seems a mere local oddity.

So the first thing to say is that all human selves, with all the powers of remembering, relating, learning, creating, and enjoying that make us who we are, survive death. By dying we are actually set free from all shrinking of personal life due to physical factors—handicaps, injuries, and deterioration of body and mind; torture and starvation; Alzheimer's disease, Down's syndrome, AIDS, and the like. This was true for both Jesus and the believing criminal to whom he said, as crucifixion drained their lives away, "Today you will be with me in paradise" (Luke 23:43). And it will be just as true for you and me.

To be sure, the ugliness and pain and aftermath of dying as we know it is the penalty of sin. For anyone unconverted in heart, who is thus already "dead in transgressions" (Eph. 2:5), dying means entering more deeply into the death state (meaning separation from that sharing with God that Scripture calls "life"). We need to be clear that as our penal substitute, Jesus "tasted" death (Heb. 2:9) in this deep sense precisely to ensure that we would never have to taste it. The natural view of his cry from the cross, "My God, my God, why have you forsaken me?" (Matt. 27:46), is that he was telling the bystanders, and through them the world, that he was undergoing deep death, as we may call it, during those dark hours, in fulfillment of prophecy (they are the first words of Psalm 22). Godforsakenness was the hell into which Jesus entered on the Cross. As Rabbi Duncan once told a class, with tears in his eyes, "It was *damnation,* and he took it *lovingly.*"

Incarnation, or the taking on of human flesh and blood and bone, along with what we call consciousness, gave the eternal Son of God capacity for this experience. "The Word [that is, Jesus] became flesh" (John 1:14). Without ceasing to be anything that he was before, he added to himself all that being human in this world involves—namely, life through a body bounded by space and time, with all the glories, limitations, and vulnerabilities that belong to everyday existence. Shakespeare, we know, acted in the plays he authored and produced, and that is a faint parallel to the co-Creator Jesus living an ordered creaturely life following a preset script within his own created world.

There are mysteries here beyond our grasp. How, for instance, did the human and divine identities mesh? How did the Son control his divine powers so as not to overstep the limits of human finiteness? But the certain fact is that as his life was a divine person's totally human life, so his dying was a divine person's totally human death.

We must keep in mind, however, that Jesus' dying was not the end of the story. His rising from the dead was a fresh exercise of the power that made the world and effected the Incarnation, leading on to the further work of power whereby the Son was glorified and enthroned, now to live as the God-Man in unbroken fellowship with his Father forever (Rom. 6:9-10). His resurrection and glorification is the prototype of what awaits all believers. His experience of dying guarantees that when it is time for us to leave this world, his loving, supportive, and sympathizing presence with us will, as William Williams's hymn puts it, "land me safe on Canaan's side." Such is God's great grace.

Theology is not for casual curiosity, but for heartfelt praise and worship. And that is never more true than when Christ's death is the theme. So Williams' contemporary, Charles Wesley, has given our question a perfect and final answer when he wrote:

'Tis mystery all! The immortal dies!
who can explore his strange design?
In vain the first-born seraph tries
to sound the depths of love divine!
'Tis mercy all! Let earth adore,
let angel minds inquire no more.

WHAT CHALLENGES DO CHRISTIANS FACE IN THE THIRD MILLENNIUM?

We're going to have to fight much more against the idea that all religions are on a par, so that they are all ways to God. Awareness of God's reality is certainly found in non-Christian faiths, and some of their ideals and disciplines are noble and humane and merit deep respect. But they lack the joy, hope, assurance, and commitment to *agape*-love which the knowledge of Jesus Christ brings. Also, their insistence that Jesus was no more than one of the world's many great teachers about religion is growing stronger.

It will take us a couple of decades to get out of the swamp of what's called *postmodernism*—a recently developed post-Christian philosophy in which relativism is all, and you have no notion of absolute truth. In the churches, we will have to be constantly speaking against that because God does speak truth, and the Christian faith is thus what Francis Schaeffer called "the truth," that is, permanent, transcultural, transhistorical *truth*—truth that abides.

We also need to recover a true understanding of human life, a sense of the greatness of the soul. We need to recover the awareness that God is more important than we are; that our future life is more important than this one; that happiness is the promise for heaven and holiness is the priority here in this world; and that nothing in this world is perfect or complete. That would give Christian people a view of the significance of our lives on a day-to-day basis, which at present, so many of us lack. Materialism and the this-worldliness which it breeds have gotten into the bones of Western believers, and it will take a lot of work in the new millennium to heal this infection.

Thank you, now, for asking these good questions.

6

KNOWING PACKER

by Wendy Murray Zoba

During my son Jon's seventh grade year, he had to wrestle two weight classes beyond his actual weight. Still, he won more matches than he lost. But during one particular match, my heart sank when he took to the mat. PeeWee Herman versus the Incredible Hulk came to mind. The buzzer sounded, and my son's opponent quickly flattened him. Yet somehow, before the interminable minute expired, Jon gathered his strength, wrested himself from his opponent's grip, and stood up.

The second period looked like the first, with the added dimension of my son having swollen eye sockets and mat burns. He flailed under the weight of his antagonist, squirming as his dwindling strength allowed, until he dislodged his foe's grip, grunted and heaved, and stood up again.

By round three the other guy looked as dazed as Jon did as they lumbered to the starting position for the third time. My son was flattened yet again, and I wouldn't have blamed him for giving up. But seizing a second wind, Jon wiggled out of the near-pin and, unbelievably, stood up again. Then, as quickly as he had been felled earlier, he flipped his opponent and had *him* flat on the mat. The crowd exploded, hoping for the upset pin, but the buzzer rang. The referee lifted the arm of my son's opponent, but everyone there recognized that something greater than a victory for one and a loss for another had transpired on that mat.

My son's match comes to my mind when I think about James Innell Packer's role in shaping contemporary evangelicalism. It helps me understand how tall this solitary man from Britain really stands, given how many times he was leveled—sometimes brutally—but kept standing up.

Packer has been well-positioned to help chart the course for the church today, both in Britain and North America. Whether it has been his discovery of the modern relevance of the Puritans, or his decision to seek ordination from the Church of England, or his forging two key Christian think tanks in Britain, or his role as the "reforming principal" at Tyndale Hall in Bristol along with his efforts to bring about a renaissance in evangelical scholarship, or his eventual emigration to Vancouver, B. C. to teach at Regent College, he has left his mark on today's Christian community. He has aroused our interest in the legacy of our spiritual forebears, the Puritans, and he has bequeathed us the ability to appropriate God-centeredness—*theology*—in a world where too often "God" is deemed irrelevant.

Once, when I announced to my sons that "Dr. Packer" would be joining us for dinner, one responded, "He's the one with the dent in his head, right?" They didn't think of him as the author of *Knowing God* or the one who has *written* more books than some people *read* in a lifetime. They remember the dent, freely showcased by Packer himself at our dinner table during a meal we had shared earlier. My boys sat riveted as he told the tale of his being chased at age seven, out of the schoolyard into the street, making—as he says it—"a violent collision with a truck, a bread van," adding, "I lost a bit of my head as a result."

J. I. Packer is a force. But he is also a "pious Puritan" (as one friend calls him), a praying Christian, a pastor/teacher, a husband and father—and to many, a friend.

FINDING TRUTH

It seemed as if the odds were against him from the get-go. Packer's modest upbringing, in a working-class family living in a rented house, did not polish him for the intellectual circles he would eventually inhabit. His father held a job at the Great Western Railway, which tendered "security but no money." Beyond that, his father, according to Packer, had been somewhat "unfitted for major responsibility," which kept his career track with the railway in the realm of the trivial, "dealing with complaints about lost luggage" and the like. He had a mental collapse at the age of fifty-two when his responsibilities increased during the war. This meant that, at times, he could be a remote and bewildering presence in the home. He eventually recovered, however, and as Packer puts it, became as "cheerful as before."

Being nearly killed by the truck introduced a new set of battles for the bookish boy from Gloucestershire. "From then on until I went to university," he recalls, "I used to move around wearing on my head an aluminum plate with a rubber pad attached around the edge. It made me more of a speckled bird than I was before."

He didn't like being a "speckled bird." He wanted to be a star cricketer. But the dent and the metal plate dashed those aspirations. So he set his hopes on the less sublime, anticipating that for his eleventh birthday, he would receive what British boys typically received on eleventh birthdays, a new bike.

His parents gave him a typewriter.

That set his course and, to some extent, his temperament. His "eggheaded" (his term) disposition coupled with the crushed head, the metal plate, and the dashed hopes, left him lonely and melancholy and displeased with his "curious features." "I don't know anyone who has a face like mine," he says. He became the easy target for the schoolyard bullies: "If they wanted someone to bully, it was very often me." He was willing to lend homework help when needed, though, even to the bullies. "If they wanted somebody to help them with their homework, again, it was very often me." He always felt on the edge of things. "There was a solitariness about my young years," he recalls.

His surprise at the typewriter instead of the bike soon "gave way to delight," Alistair McGrath notes, as he hunted-and-pecked himself into a new and satisfying world of story writing.* This summoned and sharpened his linear thinking patterns and analytical skills, which, as he says, are God-given: "God gave me a mind that always looks for the logical structure of what's being said."

But there is a downside to this kind of brilliance: "You get some shocks when you do that."

One such shock occurred during the frequent chess matches he shared with the son of a Unitarian minister. Between games, his opponent tried to sell Packer the "Unitarian bill of goods." But the presentation of Unitarian beliefs did not hold together for the linear, logical Packer, then age fifteen.

*Alistair McGrath, J. I. Packer: A Biography (Grand Rapids: Baker Book House, 1998).

"Unitarianism affirms the ethic of Jesus as the most wonderful thing since ice cream and negates the divinity of Jesus as superstition," he says. "It seemed clear to me to ask—even when I didn't know much about the contents of the Bible—if these chaps believe so much of the New Testament, why don't they believe more? If they deny something so central as the divinity of Jesus, which is clearly there, why don't they believe less? How does this position hold together?

"Not by logic," he concluded, "but by willpower."

This realization had the unexpected result of forcing him to think seriously about the Christian faith. He had grown up a churchgoer, a habit instilled by his parents. But many Anglicans, as he knew them in his day, "didn't know what they believed and didn't think it mattered," he says. So he had never given any thought to "questions of truth" about the Christian faith—that is, until the Unitarian evangelist prompted his thinking. But from then on it was a different story. "My mind had been grabbed by the question, *What is true Christianity?*"

He undertook a vigorous study of the Scriptures and other Christian writers, including C. S. Lewis, and this eventually won his intellectual assent to the truth of the historic faith. He assumed he was a Christian in every sense. Around the same time, a friend of his had gotten "soundly converted" at university and, feeling an urgency to secure Packer's salvation, he commended InterVarsity people to him. He urged Packer to seek them out once he got to Oxford for his studies. Packer's "nose for reality—*real* reality, not virtual reality," compelled him to follow his friend's advice. When he entered Corpus Christi College at Oxford in the fall of 1944, he sought out the InterVarsity people, wanting to "get in with the *real* Christians."

This, in turn, induced another shock.

Packer attended his first evangelistic preaching service of the Oxford Inter-Collegiate Christian Union (OICCU, or simply CU), and as he listened to the message, a shocking realization hit him in the form of a mental picture. He saw himself standing outside looking into a home where a party was in progress. In a spiritual sense, he understood that "they were inside and I was outside." He recognized that one *gets in* by means of a "personal transaction with the living Lord, the Lord Jesus," and that he had "never actually made that transaction."

The "pointed, perfectly ordinary, pietistic evangelistic sermon" ended with an appeal to receive the Lord Jesus as Savior. Packer recalls, "We all sang 'Just As I Am.' There's no more ordinary way of being converted than to receive the Lord while singing 'Just As I Am,' and that was it. When I went out of the church I knew I was a Christian." He abandoned Saturday night gigs playing "sloppy clarinet" for the Oxford Bandits jazz combo in deference to attending CU Bible studies.

Six weeks later he heard Basil Atkinson teach from Revelation. He was impressed by the reverence with which the teacher handled the Bible—a departure from the liberal view of Scripture he had been "stuffed up with" in the Anglicanism of his earlier teens. These two contradictory notions collided in that moment, he says, and his skepticism collapsed.

"I can still remember the feeling of surprise—and gladness— as I left the meeting because I knew that *I knew* that the Bible is the Word of God."

But the new convert soon confronted another contradiction in his faith experience.

FINDING THE PURITANS

"I was an oddity," Packer says. "I was bad at relationships, an outsider, shy, and an intellectual. I wasn't a sportsman" (the dent in his head saw to that). "Battling his way, as adolescents do," writes McGrath, the young Packer struggled with "manifold urges and surges of discontent and frustration," emotional disequilibrium, a desire for companionship, sexual longings, loneliness. On top of that, there was the added inconvenience of his operating on a higher intellectual plane than just about everybody he met, which obliged him to battle pride.

All of this had the cumulative effect of an ever-increasing isolation. "That, with my linear habit of mind, made me an eighteen year-old oddball. I was emotionally locked up."

"Let go and let God!" the evangelical ethos of the time proclaimed, which only further confounded the struggling new Christian. This was the voice of the Keswick holiness teaching that prevailed in British evangelicalism at the time. The "expository novelties," McGrath notes, espoused by the Keswick school "promised deeper spiritual enrichment," "full deliverance from sin," and a "closer relationship with Jesus Christ than anything that they had yet experienced." In fact, the teaching went, any believer who wasn't experiencing all of this "had not totally surrendered to Christ."

The contradiction tormented Packer. On the one hand, he knew that he had fully surrendered his life to the living Lord. Yet on the other hand, he was not experiencing the deliverance from sin and the victorious life that holiness teaching promised.

That's when, by a "happy accident," he found the Puritans. Having gained a reputation for bookishness, Packer had been asked to oversee the library at the OICCU shortly after his conversion. "Just out of nosiness" ("I'm a nosy person"), he started sniffing through the books. He found an edition of John Owen's *On the Mortification of Sin in Believers*—pages still uncut—and started reading. "By faith fill thy soul with a due consideration of that provision which is laid up in Jesus Christ; for this end and purpose that all thy lusts, this very lust wherewith thou art entangled, may be mortified by faith. Ponder on this, that though thou art no way able, in or by thyself, to get conquest of the distemper; though thou art even weary of contending and art utterly ready to faint; yet that there is enough in Jesus Christ to yield thee relief."

Owen became a lifeline to him, addressing, engaging, and resolving the issue of regenerate believers wrestling with sin. Writings of other Puritans he subsequently perused had a similar eye-opening, life-giving effect, dealing as they did with temperamentally based forms of human weakness. "When I read, for instance, the second part of Bunyan's *Pilgrim's Progress*, what impressed me was the way in which Mr. Greatheart, the idealized Puritan pastor who is escorting Christiana and her family to the Celestial City, picks up, as he goes along, a string of emotional cripples—Mr. Ready-to-Halt, Mr. Feeble-mind, Mr. Despondency, and his daughter Much-Afraid. From my own experience I knew a good deal already about these states of the heart, and in my ministry I have always had a special concern for the emotionally disadvantaged and the victims of what I call outsiderism, having been both myself when I was younger.

"The Puritans answered those questions that perplexed me," he says. And more than that, they introduced him to the whole range of Christian truth, wrestling with aspects of the Christian life in a rational, yet spiritually enlivened and theologically grounded way. "From the Puritans," he says, "I acquired what I didn't have from the start—that is, a sense of the importance and primacy of truth—which means theology."

MAKING INROADS

The Puritans inspired Packer to want to share the blessing both with the theologically floundering evangelical minority in Britain and with the theologically murky Church of England. To the evangelicals (a small, largely ignored minority), the Puritans' "emphasis on God-centeredness, personal discipline, humility and the primacy of the mind," writes McGrath, offered an antidote to the "pietistic goofiness" (as Packer calls it) that held sway coming out of the Keswick tradition. To the Anglicans (who composed the majority of British citizens, only 5 percent of whom were active churchgoers), the Puritans offered a theological corrective: "I knew that I had a theology that would stand and that I could deploy. One had to challenge the liberal and vague notions of Anglicanism to get them out of the way and clear the way for truth."

Packer's decision in 1947 to seek ordination in the Church of England was part of this mandate (though McGrath notes that the decision was akin to "Daniel volunteering to enter the lions' den"), as was his decision to pursue further theological training. He had taught for one academic year at Oak Hill College (1948-49), which made him aware that his gifts and disposition would be best deployed in an academic setting, and that there was a serious lack of evangelicals with doctorates in Britain (only one other evangelical that he knew of held a doctorate at the time).

As part of this mission—in the midst of preparing for ordination and pursuing his doctoral research, and with the Puritans ever on his mind—Packer launched the Puritan Studies Conferences in 1950, an annual two-day gathering for discussing papers dealing with Puritan ideas. "The Conferences proceeded on the assumption that the Puritans were to be studied as potential guides for the modern church," writes McGrath, in order to introduce to a new generation of theological students "a powerful and persuasive vision of the Christian life, in which theology, biblical exposition, spirituality and preaching were shown to be mutually indispensable."

The then well-known and revered evangelical preacher Martyn Lloyd-Jones threw his weight behind the conferences, enthusiastically endorsing and chairing them, which served as a catalyst in their subsequent success. This affiliation helped keep Packer in close proximity with his non-Anglican Free-Church brethren.

He was ordained in December 1952 (despite the examining chaplain's complaint that his theology was equivalent to "intellectual bulldozing") and assumed his first pastoral role as curate (assistant pastor) at Saint John's in Harborne. He heard no heavenly voices calling him to youth ministry, though he dutifully accompanied the Boys Brigade to camp ("I won't pretend I enjoyed it") and faithfully visited "the fish lady" (known for the bag of fish she regularly brought to church), enduring her tea. "She kept a pot of tea on the hob so that by afternoon it was scummy and tasted horrible, but that was the Birmingham way of living with tea."

But "the best of all I did," Packer recalls, "was the weekly doctrine class. All the youngish people wanted to learn about their faith, and I introduced them to their heritage. They loved it. I gave them something they discovered they wanted."

LONGINGS FULFILLED

On the academic and ministerial fronts he had been making strides toward his goals. On the personal front he remained awkward, shy, and longing for companionship. However, shortly before his ordination, the providential double booking of a friend was to turn the tide in this aspect of Packer's life. The friend asked Packer to cover for him at one of the speaking engagements, and Packer agreed, despite still feeling somewhat out of his comfort zone in situations with strangers.

His feeling of awkwardness was exacerbated when everyone in attendance, at the end of the evening, left him standing alone at the speaker's table while they mingled casually with one another.

Everyone, that is, except a young nursing student who redressed this "terrible rudeness." "I was affronted by the fact that everybody else around me was ignoring the speaker," says Kit, Packer's wife of forty-six years. "We Welsh people generally try to make strangers at ease."

Kit left her comfort zone, too, to welcome the visiting speaker who stood awkwardly before her. He spoke, she recounts, "remarkably like my minister, Dr. Martyn Lloyd-Jones."

That first meeting with Kit Mullett left J. I. Packer tossing sleepless in his bed. "I couldn't get her out of my mind," he says. When he got up in the middle of that sleepless night to read Proverbs 31 (the account of the godly woman), he felt as if the writer had Kit in mind. "She seemed to be there."

Kit possessed all those qualities that he, in his bookish way, seemed to lack. She was practical, relational, lively, and independent. He liked the "individuality" he saw in her on their first walk in the wood when she took her shoes off.

She's Welsh; he's English. She highlights that point. When they take walks together, she meanders (still sometimes barefoot), carrying binoculars, watching the chickadees, and tracing the flight of the bald eagle; he bolts, wanting to get there and back again. He keeps his shoes on.

She moves comfortably into "the debating mode" (Packer notes: "She's not sure she can see coherence in my position on women in ministry"). He demurs: "I'm an analyst. I'm not a debater."

"When he took an interest, I was surprised," Kit recalls. "I still am, actually."

They courted for eighteen months "under the eye of my vicar" and paid for their own wedding in July of 1954, the week after he turned in his 500-page dissertation on Richard Baxter.

So his longings for companionship were filled to overflowing in his new bride, and Packer grew more sure of his mission and mandate. He left his pastoral duties at Saint John's, and in 1955, assumed the position of assistant lecturer, soon to become senior tutor, at Tyndale Hall in Bristol.

LIFTER OF DROOPING HEADS

At this time, a young American crusade evangelist named Billy Graham brought his crusades to Britain (1954 and 1955) and ignited evangelical fires. Christian unions were expanding in the universities at a rate heretofore unseen. This surge in popular evangelical enthusiasms unsettled the Anglican establishment. Canon H. K. Luce, headmaster of Durham School, wrote an article in which he posted the question (cited by McGrath): "Is it not time that our religious leaders made it plain that while they respect, or even admire, Dr. Graham's sincerity and personal power, they cannot regard fundamentalism as likely to issue in anything but disillusionment and disaster for educated men and women in this twentieth century?"

Packer answered that question. He took pen in hand and offered "the definitive evangelical response" in his first book, *"Fundamentalism" and the Word of God* (1958). In that book, Packer demonstrated cogently and rationally that authentic evangelicalism, contrary to Luce's remarks, carried all the intellectual rigor that the liberals presumed to be their own special domain, while simultaneously turning their flawed argumentation back upon them. As Valentine Cunningham put it in the *Pelican Record:* "It felt good to have Packer on one's side, this gangly bespectacled exegete with the Gloucestershire burr in his voice, a sort of John Arlott of biblical commentary, running up to bowl his devastating slow left-arm deliveries."

Packer says that his response was simply "to outflank the criticisms by showing that they applied to the critics much more than they applied to those at whom they were first directed."

Robert Horn, former editor of the *Evangelical Times*, said that the book lifted the "drooping heads" of a whole generation of young people. He "made doctrine exciting," as one observer noted, showing the skeptics that Scripture could be trusted after all and reassuring the pietists that reason could be their friend. The book established Packer as the voice for a credible, intellectually rigorous, yet soundly orthodox, evangelicalism.

Making strides in his mission, he undertook another project similar to his Puritan Conferences, which were by then thriving. Just as these offered a venue for Puritan thought to infiltrate British evangelicalism, his next brainchild, Latimer House, launched in 1961, was Packer's means to create a venue for Anglican *evangelicals* to make their voices heard within their denomination.

Packer wanted to revive "authentic Anglicanism," a heritage, he says, that had been in eclipse since the twentieth century began. "The shapers of Anglicanism were evangelicals— Cranmer, the Puritans, the Clapham sect, Wilberforce, Ryle," he says. "I wanted to reestablish it in its own heritage." So in 1961 Packer left Bristol to become librarian (later, warden) at Latimer House.

On the home front, the Packers had settled into family life with their three children, Naomi, Ruth, and Martin. "Kit wanted and got animals," Packer notes, including (at one point or another) hamsters, rabbits, white mice, cats, and dogs.

Packer enjoyed his young children, though Kit recalls that at times—especially when he was writing a book—"he wasn't always with us." Packer left home management in the capable hands of his wife, though he says, "I invested more of myself in parenting than my father invested in me."

On other fronts, however, Packer was soon to enter a season of testing and heartache. With the rise of the World Council of Churches in the sixties, being affiliated with a denomination like the Church of England became suspect. Some feared that the WCC would become "a 'superchurch' run from Geneva," as Packer puts it, and they began advocating abandoning the denomination to form a separate evangelical alliance. Packer's friend and Puritan Conference partner, Martyn Lloyd-Jones, became the most outspoken advocate of this. At the initial gathering of the Second National Assembly of Evangelicals (October 1966), organized by the Evangelical Alliance, Lloyd-Jones "issued what was widely understood to be a passionate call for evangelicals within the mainstream churches to 'come out' and, in effect, form a denomination of their own," McGrath writes. John Stott, a well-known Anglican evangelical who was chairing the session, feared that the message might spark a mass exodus on the part of the younger, impressionable evangelical leaders in attendance. So Stott "broke the ordinary rules of procedure," says Packer, and intervened to affirm that evangelicals could and should remain within their denominations in order to help bring about renewal from within. "It started a great row that didn't die down," Packer says.

This unexpected turn resulted in a rift in British evangelicalism over whether evangelicals should remain within the Church of England. So the gathering that was supposed to "serve the purpose to advance the cause of unity and viable strategies for keeping evangelicalism alive in Britain" had the opposite effect.

TROUBLE THREE TIMES OVER

Packer told me once: "Like a good pietist I've always wanted peace, and like Richard Baxter I've been involved with trouble, trouble, trouble all the way." This was never more true than the season he entered in the early seventies, what I would call the opening bell of J. I. Packer's extraordinary match. Several forces converged that set the conditions wherein Packer found himself, at some points, scrambling to save his academic career, and at other points, groping for his place in the British evangelical arena.

By the late sixties, the unity between Anglican evangelicals and the Free-Church brethren was disintegrating; a "charismatic tidal wave" (as Packer calls it) that emphasized experience over intellect deluged the British evangelical scene and had begun to erode some of the theological underpinnings Packer had labored to establish; and Packer himself was itching for new challenges, sensing that Latimer House, now thriving, no longer demanded his leadership.

The first round, to continue the wrestling metaphor, commenced with Packer's formal disfellowshiping by Martyn Lloyd-Jones in 1970. The two had not seen eye-to-eye on the role of evangelicals within Anglicanism, and Lloyd-Jones had hoped that Packer would eventually see things his way. (Once, when Kit went to Lloyd-Jones for a pastoral visit, her concerns were overridden by his urging her to persuade her husband to come over to his side. Packer had been his "blue-eyed boy," says Kit.)

The break occurred as a result of a book Packer had written with other Anglicans, two of whom were Anglo-Catholics, in an effort to overturn the "Methodist union scheme" (a movement to unite the denomination with the Methodists). From Lloyd-Jones's perspective, Packer had gone too far in collaborating with the Anglo-Catholics, though Packer maintains that Lloyd-Jones "read into the book a good deal that it hadn't said."

Lloyd-Jones also abruptly ended what had become two decades of flourishing Puritan Conferences. Packer, in turn, was unceremoniously sacked by other committees and boards, including the editorial board of *The Evangelical Magazine*. McGrath writes that a "leading independent evangelical went so far as to advance the view that Packer could 'no longer be regarded as an evangelical.'"

Lloyd-Jones, Packer reflects, was "the greatest man I ever knew." But he was also inviting evangelicals "on a road that led to nowhere." ("Great men can make great mistakes.") Packer was committed to going the long haul within the denomination. "Whatever anything else Jim was, he was an Anglican," says Kit. "He would never desert the Church of England." Despite his personal affection for Lloyd-Jones, Packer never felt that "the Free-Church men could ever grab the tiller" in his quest to renew the church.

Still another crisis loomed, sounding the buzzer for round two. Theological schools in Britain faced a steady decrease of candidates for ordination, and Packer, having left Latimer

House to assume the role of principal of Tyndale Hall in Bristol in 1970, had undertaken an aggressive plan to increase student membership and assemble a sterling faculty there (hence his recognition as the "reforming principal").

To maintain viability, proposals to merge some colleges were introduced. Tyndale, Packer's college, remained under a threatening cloud. "Theological colleges across England, irrespective of their theological tradition, found themselves plunged into fierce and bitter battles for survival," writes McGrath.

John Stott and others, wanting to ensure the survival of *evangelical* colleges, submitted in September 1970 an unofficial report proposing the consolidation of the three Bristol colleges: Tyndale, Clifton, and Dalton House (a women's college). The commission overseeing the mergers countered, in October, with a different recommendation: All schools in Bristol would be shut down, with Clifton joining Wycliffe Hall in Oxford, and Packer's Tyndale joining Saint John's in Nottingham.

This was a devastating blow to Packer. He had worked hard and paid a high price for forging a new vision for theological training within Anglicanism and had only just begun to turn the tide at Tyndale. He recognized that if this merger with Saint John's proceeded, which neither school relished, his vision and leadership would be disenfranchised, since Saint John's stood as the stronger, more self-sufficient of the two schools.

Following Packer's lead, Tyndale responded in January 1971 that a move to Nottingham was unworkable. The commission, in turn, countered that, fine, Tyndale would be *closed*.

Shock gave way to disbelief, which gave way to outrage. Packer found himself in the middle of a firestorm trying to save his college; and by now, the students themselves had entered the fray trying to overturn the decision. The General Synod of the Church of England debated the issue and ultimately, in February, offered Tyndale a reprieve: "In the opinion of the House of Bishops, the continuation of training for ordinands at Bristol is only possible if Tyndale Hall, Clifton and Dalton . . . agree to amalgamate on the Clifton site."

Hence, Trinity College was born and an evangelical presence in Bristol was saved. But Packer's troubles weren't over. The leadership question for the newly formed school had to be addressed. A triumvirate arrangement was considered the most desirable, with one member from each college assuming a leadership position. Packer was recommended, for obvious reasons, to represent Tyndale in the triumvirate.

But things got more complicated. In the planning sessions between the potential leaders, Packer unintentionally alienated the Clifton leadership, who felt Packer was dictating the terms. He wasn't. They probably took offense at Packer's linear habit of mind and style of communication. (Once he starts a thought he simply cannot stop until the thought has been carried through to its logical conclusion. There's no interrupting him.)

Fearing a Tyndale takeover, they stalled further negotiations, derailing the merger. In the end, Packer was vindicated by the bishop, who intervened and saved the merger; but the new arrangement carried the proviso that J. I. Packer *not* be given any significant leadership role. So rather than serving as dean of studies (part of the triumvirate), Packer was offered the position of associate principal.

EDGED OUT

Gerald Bray commends McGrath for correctly "expos[ing] the moral void at the heart of so much Anglican evangelicalism." He adds, "Packer, as theologian, was a threat to people like that. The only surprise is that they were prepared to tolerate him at all."

Bray highlights the fact that ten years later, after Packer and his friend and colleague Alec Motyer (who filled the Tyndale triumvirate slot) had left, "Trinity sank to a depth which even the men of Clifton may not have envisaged.

"There are many who remember the Packer-Motyer years as the golden age of Bristol."

So it wasn't all bad news for J. I. Packer. As associate principal, he took advantage of increased opportunities for travel and writing. *Knowing God* was published in 1973, winning Packer immediate international acclaim, particularly in North America. This, in turn, resulted in his being asked to participate in controversies here. One such conflict that erupted in the United States was a ferment dubbed "the battle for the Bible," for which Packer was invited to offer input as an objective outsider (for once).

He participated in summit meetings and, later, helped draft key expositions for the International Council on Biblical Inerrancy (ICBI), which he also helped found in 1977. Packer assisted American evangelicals in navigating this delicate debate, leading them to middle ground whereby they could fully embrace "inerrancy" (though Packer prefers to characterize Scripture by the positive terms "totally true, totally trustworthy") without sacrificing common sense and adopting the ultraliteralistic approach advocated by some, in the attempt to reconcile apparent inconsistencies in the gospel accounts—like the suggestion that there may have been six, not three, denials of Jesus by Peter.

So doors were opening for him across the puddle. Back in England, however, he was becoming gradually more marginalized. The Church of England's Doctrine Committee, of which Packer was a member, published a statement that treated orthodox Christian understanding of the person and work of Christ as "an option." This enraged the ordinary Anglicans who wondered how a theological stance could be hijacked by so few. And it exacerbated the criticism by non-Anglican evangelicals who felt Packer had surrendered too much by staying with the denomination. Packer, for his part, felt that "the dice were loaded" against them, since, as McGrath notes, the evangelicals were hopelessly outnumbered on the committee.

On another front, his friend and fellow Anglican evangelical, John Stott, was charting a different course for British evangelicalism than that which Packer had envisioned. Stott orchestrated central conferences for leaders to gather for fellowship and refreshment, with the hope that the inspiration would trickle down into their churches. Packer felt that igniting evangelistic fervor in the context of these conferences would diminish the urgency in local congregations. It seemed to be merely a matter of differing emphases, but the overall effect of this, along with these other difficulties, left Packer feeling "the odd man out."

"In the 1970s," he reflects, "I hadn't got any kind of leadership role or direct hearing for the things I wanted to say among evangelicals any more than I did in my Anglican circles. I don't think I ever lapsed into bitterness, but it has on occasion made me wonder what good I am, really, to the Christian world in the short term."

A NEW TURN

Round three.

"Packer left this universe in 1979 for a new life at Regent College, Vancouver," Bray writes, "and Dr. McGrath presents this as a wider opportunity given to him to develop his preaching and teaching ministry." A notion, Bray continues, that is "the exact opposite of the one generally held by Dr. Packer's admirers in England.

"What we were looking for was a new Charles Hodge, or even just a new Louis Berkhof, but what we got was *Knowing God*," he says. "It has to be recorded that this has been the expectation of the English friends and admirers, and that so far we have felt let down."

Not all Brits concur with Bray's assessment, to which McGrath's book attests. And feeling "let down" would hardly describe the sentiment of J. I Packer's friends and admirers in North America. He thrived at Regent ("without any sort of negative vibes"), and Regent has flourished because of his being there. "In the mid-1970s, Regent was a tiny institution, using borrowed rooms; by the end of the 1980s, Regent was the largest graduate institution of theological education in the region," writes McGrath.

Regent placed Packer in a position to assert a voice in just about every theological discussion that has emerged in contemporary North American evangelicalism—from the role of women, to the function of the Holy Spirit, to the destiny of those who die without Christ. The most recent of these has been his critical role in Evangelicals and Catholics Together (ECT), wherein Packer has helped navigate both sides of this initiative onto common theological ground without diminishing the points of disagreement.

It should be noted that he has also been disfellowshiped by some American evangelicals for his participation in ECT—despite his obvious and vigorous commitment to evangelical faith and unwillingness to give any ground on critical theological matters. He has played a key role in facilitating the sense of unity and cooperation that has prevailed in ECT—his off-the-cuff, after-hours comment to Catholic theologian Richard John Neuhaus, that the papacy is "a grotesque institution" notwithstanding.

In the meantime, he continues to generate an unrelenting arsenal of books, pamphlets, and articles—writing a book a year since coming to Regent. ("In 1995 three Packer books were published together and I got up to speed.") His books have sold almost 3 million copies (*Knowing God*, 1.5 million in and of itself), and he has earned the status of being the best-selling author in British Columbia.

At my dinner table not too long ago, Packer couldn't stay his tears when Handel's "For Unto Us a Child Is Born," from *Messiah*, played in the background. That is because, as Kit says it, "his devotion to the Lord is the reason for everything he's done.

His writing, his preaching, his lecturing, his *living* are all centered on the Lord."

And his love for the church is why Packer prefers the verb form of theology—to "theologize." He told me once that classical jazz is like the church—a lively, masterful interplay and synergy of members, orchestrated by the Holy Spirit for creating the music of heaven.

When the painful rifts have occurred over the years, he has grieved less for his personal losses and more because, as Kit puts it, "the church is hurt and the Lord is hurt." That is why, ten years after their estrangement in 1970, Packer wrote his friend and colleague, Martyn Lloyd-Jones, asking to visit him on his forthcoming trip to England. Lloyd-Jones, who had been ill, encouraged him to come.

"I never saw him," Packer says. "He died before I could get there. It didn't make a great deal of difference," he says. "There's always heaven."

Yes, heaven. Packer's thoughts are high and wide, though his feet are firmly planted here. "I want to see a focused vision of spiritual maturity—the expansion of the soul is the best phrase I can use for it. That is, a renewed sense of the momentousness of being alive, the sheer bigness and awesomeness of being a human being living in God's world with light, with grace, with wisdom, with responsibility, with biblical truth.

"I judge rightly or wrongly," he says, "that as a generation, most of us are pygmies as compared with the great-souled Christians of earlier days, the Athanasiuses, the Luthers, the Anselms—people like Whitefield, Wesley, and Edwards. They were, by the grace of God, bigger people than most of us are."

The Oxford don, Valentine Cunningham, writes, "Packer

121

stands for an arresting and influential blend of spirituality and theological hardheadedness." The operative word there is *stands*. Like my son who gutted his way through an uneven match, achieving something greater than a victory, so the testimony of J. I. Packer transcends the total sum of blows leveled against him. The boy who decades ago nearly died being chased into the street, and who came back later to help bullies with their homework, today seems bigger than most of us.